Teen Guide to
Starting a Business

Gail Snyder

ReferencePoint
Press®

San Diego, CA

About the Author
Gail Snyder is a freelance writer and advertising copywriter who has written more than twenty books for young readers. She lives in Chalfont, Pennsylvania, with her husband, Hal Marcovitz.

For more information, contact:
ReferencePoint Press, Inc.
PO Box 27779
San Diego, CA 92198
www.ReferencePointPress.com

Picture Credits:
Cover: iStockphoto.com/annebaek
 4: Maury Aaseng
18: Depositphotos
42: Depositphotos
53: Shutterstock.com/Pressmaster

LIBRARY OF CONGRESS CATALOGING-IN-PUBLICATION DATA

Names: Snyder, Gail, author.
Title: Teen guide to starting a business / by Gail Snyder.
Description: San Diego, CA : ReferencePoint Press, Inc., 2017. | Series:
  Guide to finances | Audience: Grade 9 to 12. | Includes bibliographical
  references and index.
Identifiers: LCCN 2016004754 (print) | LCCN 2016014932 (ebook) | ISBN
  9781682820889 (hardback) | ISBN 9781682820896 (eBook)
Subjects: LCSH: New business enterprises--Juvenile literature. |
  Entrepreneurship--Juvenile literature. | Small
  business--Management--Juvenile literature. | CYAC: Vocational guidance.
Classification: LCC HD62.5 .S669 2017 (print) | LCC HD62.5 (ebook) | DDC
  658.1/10835--dc23
LC record available at https://lccn.loc.gov/2016004754

Contents

Shifts in Entrepreneurial Activity, by Age

In the decade between 2003 and 2013, the share of entrepreneurs in the United States grew most among people between the ages of 45 and 64. Statistics from the Kauffman Foundation, an organization whose focus is education and entrepreneurship, show that the percentage of entrepreneurs rose during that period by 4.8 percent and 4.7 percent (respectively) among ages 45 to 54 and ages 55 to 64. According to the foundation's report, the biggest drop in share of entrepreneurs during that decade (5.8 percent) occurred among people between the ages of 35 and 44.

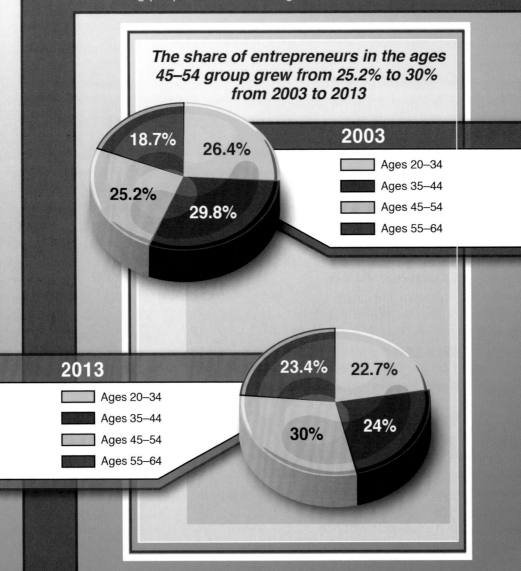

The share of entrepreneurs in the ages 45–54 group grew from 25.2% to 30% from 2003 to 2013

2003

18.7% 26.4% 25.2% 29.8%

- Ages 20–34
- Ages 35–44
- Ages 45–54
- Ages 55–64

2013

23.4% 22.7% 30% 24%

- Ages 20–34
- Ages 35–44
- Ages 45–54
- Ages 55–64

Source: Dane Stangler, "Infographic: Kauffman Index of Entrepreneurial Activity, 1996–2013," Kauffman Foundation, April 9, 2014. www.kauffman.org.

Chapter One

What Does It Take to Own a Business?

Many people dream about owning their own businesses. As many as 39 percent of people who work for others have expressed the desire to be their own bosses, according to a 2014 University of Phoenix School of Business survey. Moreover, the wish to be one's own boss especially resonates with people in their twenties who took part in the survey. Half of them thought the idea of running their own companies was highly appealing.

It isn't hard to understand why. During tough economic times, people who work for others can find themselves out of work through no fault of their own. This may occur when companies downsize, merge with other corporations, outsource jobs to foreign countries where labor is cheap, or simply go out of business. Job security is never guaranteed—even for hardworking, reliable employees.

However, those who take the plunge and open their own businesses would do well to know that success is not guaranteed. According to the US Small Business Administration (SBA), 50 percent of small businesses fail during their first five years. Further, only about 33 percent of businesses that make it into their fifth year are around long enough to celebrate their tenth anniversaries.

And yet new businesses open all the time. There is not much of a pattern to these start-ups. While some owners have new ideas, many do not. While some have a lot of experience, many do not. While some start with a lot of money, most do not. While many are adults, some are not. What these businesses have in common is a person with a commitment to imagine the business before it is created and the drive to follow through with its execution.

Traits of a Business Owner

Running a business is a lot different from being an employee who works for someone else. Although many employees are devoted to their jobs and put in a great deal of time and energy, the primary role of an employee is to show up and leave on time, complete the assigned tasks, and collect a paycheck. At the end of the day, many employees can walk away from their jobs and not have to think about them until the next workday rolls around. The role of the business owner is much more involved. Business owners are responsible for finding customers; making certain they are happy; living up to deadlines; and meeting expenses that include payroll, buying equipment and supplies, and paying taxes. In a small business, the business owner is also responsible for hiring, firing, and managing employees.

Why would anyone want to take on all of those roles? The typical business owner, sometimes called an entrepreneur, tends to like the idea of being in charge, making decisions, guiding a company to succeed and thrive—and is willing to do whatever it takes to make

From Dishwasher to Restaurant Owner

Many high school students have part-time jobs. Amol Kohli of Voorhees, New Jersey, began working for Friendly's, a restaurant chain, at age fifteen. He washed dishes, scooped ice cream, served as a host seating customers, and worked as a cook. After graduating high school, Kohli earned a degree from Drexel University in Philadelphia, where he majored in finance and marketing.

Using the skills he learned at Drexel as well as on the job at Friendly's, Kohli has gone on to buy his own Friendly's restaurants. By 2015, at age twenty-seven, Kohli owned nine restaurants, overseeing some seven hundred full- and part-time employees as well as a payroll of more than $3 million. Kohli was able to buy his first Friendly's by using his own savings, borrowing $50,000 from his parents, and obtaining a bank loan.

Graham R. Laub, an attorney who helps Kohli negotiate the purchases of his restaurants, says it is clear his client learned some valuable lessons about work during his years as a cook and dishwasher. In an interview with the *Philadelphia Inquirer*, Laub said, "He's got a great work ethic. He's a hustler and he's very driven. That's what you need to be successful."

that happen. The ideal entrepreneur possesses the desire to succeed and the ability to manage time well. Also, entrepreneurs recognize when they need help and are not afraid to ask for it. Entrepreneurs are good problem solvers. They communicate well and are leaders others want to follow.

People who possess these qualities can also make first-rate employees. But what really sets those destined to be their own boss apart from excellent employees is a tolerance for risk and a passion they must explore. Passion also plays a role in maintaining the total commitment it takes to surmount obstacles. And passion personifies the entrepreneur's commitment to customers, who can often easily tell, from their personal interaction with the owner, if that owner truly cares about the business he or she is running. "You have to be passionate about it. Otherwise it's not worth doing. Owning your own business is not easy and it's not going to make you rich quick. You're going to be in it for the long haul so it's got to be something you love," says Mollie Breault-Binaghi in the SBA publication *Young Entrepreneurs: An Essential Guide to Starting Your Own Business*. Breault-Binaghi should know. By age twenty-five she already owned two businesses—one specializing in website design and the other offering graphic design and printing services.

Commitment in Time

Running a business can be incredibly time consuming. Business owners may find themselves working from early in the morning to late at night. Clients, suppliers, employees, and others may call at any time, day or night. Emergencies must be addressed when they happen—even if they happen at midnight. Entrepreneurs may be forced to sacrifice leisure activities, time with their families, and even sleep when the need arises. "Running a business is, in a word, busy," says Michael Morris, a professor of marketing at the University of Florida and author of the book *A Practical Guide to Entrepreneurship*. "There is a lot to do and, in the early days, probably only you to do it."

A report by the business management software firm Sage found that 40 percent of business owners work more hours a week than they used to; also, 40 percent take less vacation time than they used to. In an interview with *USA Today*, Katie Hellmuth Martin, cofounder of the business promotions firm Tin Shingle, says time demands of growing a new business often force entrepreneurs to make personal sacrifices. She says they may find themselves in damaged relationships with friends and family members and even face physical ills if they work too hard and too long. Moreover, she warns, when business owners take calls or answer e-mails late at night, they may send signals to clients, employees, and others that they are available anytime, day or night. "If you're doing too much work, you might be creating false expectations about what you can do," she says.

> **"Owning your own business is not easy and it's not going to make you rich quick. You're going to be in it for the long haul so it's got to be something you love."**
>
> **—Business owner Mollie Breault-Binaghi.**

But some entrepreneurs are willing to sacrifice leisure time for success. In 2008, at age nineteen, Seth Priebatsch founded Scvngr, a Boston, Massachusetts, company that provides smartphone apps for players to participate in real-world scavenger hunts. Within three years the company grew to be worth $100 million. Scvngr employs more than eighty people and has sold its applications to 1.5 million users. Priebatsch says he could not have achieved success if he hadn't devoted most of his waking hours to growing the business. "I get almost as much done outside normal office hours as during them," Priebatsch told the *Entrepreneur* website. "I'll interview [job applicants] on Saturdays, late at night, early in the morning. . . . During startup, I think you have the choice of being productive or having a social life, and I've chosen being productive."

Learning from Failure

One important trait found among entrepreneurs is the ability to learn from failure. Business owners must be able to view failure as a learning experience instead of a disaster. One entrepreneur who learned from failure is Rand Fishkin. By age twenty-five, Fishkin built a successful cyberconsulting firm—Moz. This was his second attempt at entrepreneurship; his first effort, a marketing firm, failed and left him more than $500,000 in debt. Looking back, Fishkin concluded that he had surrounded himself with employees who were loath to disagree with him or offer their own ideas that would help grow the business.

> "During startup, I think you have the choice of being productive or having a social life, and I've chosen being productive."
>
> —Business owner Seth Priebatsch.

Learning from failure, Fishkin established Moz, which helps companies enhance their visibility on the Internet. When seeking employees for Moz, Fishkin says he always looks for workers who are not hesitant to question his judgment. He told the website Business Insider, "Failure—a very harsh failure—taught me you cannot surround yourself with 'yes men' (or 'yes women'). Disagreement and conflict are healthy. They create stronger, better decisions, and more exploration of the risks and opportunities."

By 2014, just two years after founding Moz, the company signed up more than twenty thousand clients, recording an annual income of $30 million. Says Fishkin,

"It's a long, painful journey, but those early failures (and even failures we make every week these days) have helped us continue to get better."

Taking Advantage of Personal Connections

New business owners face the enormous task of trying to launch and grow their new enterprises with very little help from others. Most will not be able to hire many employees, if they are, indeed, able to hire any workers at all. Certainly, it is not unusual for new business owners to work without salaries for at least several months until their ventures start earning profits. Nevertheless, new business owners may find themselves in need of help. In fact, there are many resources they can tap as they grow their businesses.

For example, most people already have networks of relationships in place that could benefit them in many ways. Family members, friends, neighbors, former teachers, and colleagues form social networks that can help get a new business off to a secure start. These people may be willing to lend advice, manpower, or assets—such as a pickup truck—that may have been otherwise out of reach for the new owner of, say, a lawn care business.

At age seventeen, Emily Bergson-Shilcock started her own business, Destination of Independence. She opened a store in Ardmore, Pennsylvania, selling products for disabled people. These products included large shoehorns, devices that help with turning keys and holding playing cards, and scissors designed for people with physical limitations. To launch the business, she used $1,000 of her own money while borrowing $3,000 from her parents. Her father helped her outfit the store, building shelves and display cases,

The Option of Freelancing

People who have skills others are willing to pay for can go into business for themselves as freelancers. This shortcut to independence is taken by those who can, for example, write for publication; design websites, logos, and packaging; and perform bookkeeping functions for small companies.

Freelancers are attractive to the businesses that hire them because they do not have the expenses associated with employing them, with no need to pay for health insurance or provide them with desks or equipment. They pay only for the hours or projects the freelancer works on. From the freelancers' points of view, the arrangement allows them to work full or part time, usually from home, choose whom they work for, and set their own hourly or project rates.

There are, however, many downsides to freelancing. Sometimes freelancers can have more work than they can comfortably handle but may not want to turn jobs down because there will be other times when work is slow. With no coworkers to interact with, being a freelancer may not be ideal for those who thrive on social interaction. Also, freelancers can find themselves competing with people from other countries whose fees may be dramatically lower.

while her mother designed brochures. Her sisters, Amanda and Julia, and brother, Nicholas, volunteered their time in the store, helping stock merchandise on the shelves and filling orders. "My family was very supportive in helping me translate my dream into a reality," Bergson-Shilcock told Frances A. Karnes and Suzanne M. Bean, authors of the book *Girls and Young Women Entrepreneurs*.

Measured Growth

New business owners need to know that whatever enterprise they take on, they will invariably start small and that it could take years to grow their companies. That notion might not appeal to the new business owner who dreams of conquering the corporate world overnight. A clear example of a small company that found enormous success through careful and measured growth is Ben & Jerry's, which earns more than $500 million a year selling its quirky ice-cream flavors. Ben & Jerry's started in 1978 when two friends—Ben Cohen and Jerry Greenfield—established the company in a former gas station in Burlington, Vermont. At the time, both were twenty-six years old.

Starting with just $12,000 to establish the business—$4,000 of their own money and $8,000 in borrowed funds—Cohen and Greenfield grew their business slowly, just selling ice cream directly to customers out of the Burlington store. After a few years of developing flavors, the partners moved up to delivering pints to grocery stores throughout New England. Recalled Cohen in an interview with the *Washington Post*, "Come winter, more money was going out than was coming in, and we didn't really have any cash reserves. We weren't making as much money as we had hoped in the summer, either, because we were over-scooping. We couldn't bring ourselves to scoop smaller portions, because customers wanted the big scoops."

Slowly, though, their unique concoctions helped them build a dedicated customer base. Greenfield said the turning point in transforming Ben & Jerry's from a small company into a big business probably occurred in 1984 when the partners concocted chocolate chip cookie dough ice cream, finding the flavor to be enormously popular. Asked how they grew the company, Greenfield replied:

> It definitely didn't happen overnight. If there was one moment to point back to, though, it was probably the invention of chocolate chip cookie dough ice cream—that really captured people's imaginations, and it came about because we had started baking homemade cookies on site along with the homemade ice cream at the store in Vermont. One day, the baker and the ice cream maker got together, and the baker said, "Why don't you try some of this cookie dough in the ice cream?"

The company's careful and measured step-by-step climb into prosperity serves as an example of how a slow and methodical approach can help make a small business into a success.

Overcoming Obstacles

The obstacles to starting a business are many. Business owners surveyed in the 2014 University of Phoenix study identified some of the obstacles as not having enough money (67 percent), lacking education or training about business (33 percent), lacking a viable business idea (30 percent), not having the time to run a business (22 percent), and not possessing the ability to manage others (17 percent). Nevertheless, thousands of entrepreneurs start new businesses every year. They are able to find ways to surmount the obstacles standing in their way. As long as they possess the passion to succeed and are willing to learn from their mistakes, prospective entrepreneurs may find friends, teachers, industry veterans, and other experts willing to provide help getting a new business off the ground.

Chapter Two

Picking the Right Business

Kevin Plank didn't know much about business, but he knew a lot about football. In the early 1990s he played fullback for the University of Maryland as a walk-on, meaning he won a place on the team without having been offered an athletic scholarship as a high school player. Smaller than many of his teammates, Plank compensated by hustling a bit more than everyone else.

During practice, Plank noticed he was forced to carry extra weight because his cotton T-shirts absorbed his sweat—he even weighed his undergarments after practice and learned he was carrying an extra 3 pounds (1.4 kg). Plank wondered whether T-shirts and other athletic garments could be made of materials that would wick moisture rather than absorb it. He found a fabric store near campus, explained what he wanted, and walked out with a bolt of synthetic fabric. Next, he found a tailor who stitched together some sample T-shirts, which he handed out to his teammates. After the first practice, the players raved about their new garments, finding themselves much more mobile because they didn't have to carry extra weight. After practice, the synthetic fabric T-shirts weighed just 7 ounces (198 g).

After graduation, Plank went into the athletic apparel business, creating T-shirts out of nylon and similar synthetic fabrics. He ran up credit card debt totaling $40,000 but soon started filling orders for colleges such as Georgia Tech and North Carolina State. And then the Atlanta Falcons placed an order for apparel. Today Plank's company, Under Armour, is valued at some $3 billion and sells athletic apparel to customers around the globe. He told Amy Wilkinson, author of *The Creator's Code: The Six Essential Skills of Extraordinary Entrepreneurs*, "What defines our brand is . . . this walk-on mentality, that there is nothing that can stop me, there is nothing that can prevent me from moving forward and being successful."

> "There is nothing that can stop me, there is nothing that can prevent me from moving forward and being successful."
>
> —Business owner Kevin Plank.

Plank's story illustrates the success an entrepreneur can find if he or she picks the right business. Certainly, Plank's knowledge about football and the rigors of practice helped him realize the enormous market that awaited an entrepreneur who could provide athletic apparel composed of synthetic fabrics.

Product-Based Businesses

While few entrepreneurs find themselves on the road to creating businesses valued in the billions of dollars, they can nevertheless find success by picking the business that best fits their interests and skill sets. In creating athletic apparel made of synthetic fabrics, Plank brought a new product to the market. Ideas for products often come from the entrepreneurs' life experiences, such as the ones Plank found on the practice field.

Products can range from the simple to the complex—entrepreneurs with the ability to write computer code can develop their own smartphone applications. Others with artistic skills can make and sell their own jewelry or clothing. The potential to develop a new product is limited only by the entrepreneur's creativity, intelligence, and skills.

The idea for Mindy Ann Nunez's product-based business, which she began in high school, came from her father. He owned a store in New Orleans, Louisiana, and observed that vinyl stickers sold very well. The stickers, which featured logos and other designs, could be easily attached and removed from car windows and other surfaces. Mindy Ann's father suggested to his daughter that she could make and sell her own original designs. Starting with no knowledge about making decals, Mindy Ann and her father researched what she needed to get started. Next, her father lent her the money to buy the decal-making equipment. The business, which Mindy Ann named M.A.N. Designs, proved profitable. Soon after becoming proficient at creating decals, Mindy Ann aimed to expand her products to include signs and printed advertisements. She told Frances A. Karnes and Suzanne M. Bean, "I've started focusing on signs and lettering instead of just decals. Although the decals still sell quite well, I'm considering moving into the competitive field of advertising and sign making. . . . This field looks very promising."

Service Businesses Solve Problems

People whose talents lack a measure of creativity or the skills required to otherwise make new products should not feel frozen out of entrepreneurship. They can always consider establishing businesses that are service based. Service businesses save customers time and/or money, enable them to find somebody to perform a task they

Service-oriented businesses vary in complexity. A house-painting business requires certain skills and specific equipment, while a tutoring business requires knowledge but little in the way of equipment.

can't do for themselves, or provide customers with a way out of doing tasks they do not enjoy.

Examples of service-based enterprises could be as simple as lawn care, pet sitting, or tutoring. A higher set of skills is required for people who open their own plumbing, carpentry, or house-painting businesses. Some huge corporations earn their profits as service providers, such as United Parcel Service (UPS), which delivers more than 15 million packages a day; or American Airlines, which flies some three hundred thousand passengers to their destinations each day.

When contemplating a service business, entrepreneurs need to pinpoint what types of customers they want to attract. As they search for ideas, they can focus on the type of customers they would enjoy working with. Some options include young parents and children, the elderly, homeowners, or pet owners. As they think about the type of people who would compose their customer base, they would also do well to think about the skill sets they could offer those customers.

Artists—both professional and amateur—make up the customer base that Angelo Sotira had in mind in 2000 when, at age nineteen, he cofounded the social networking site DeviantArt. The site enables artists to create accounts and sell their work, buy merchandise, view other people's art, and provide commentary on art-related themes. Since the site went online, some 30 million artists have created accounts, uploading more than one hundred thousand images per day. Sotira says he conceived the idea for the site as a response to computer users who were skinning their software—meaning altering software to add individual creative touches to the graphics and animation available in commercially obtained programs. Sotira realized the skinners, who regard themselves as artists, wanted a social networking platform to show off their creations. Soon after establishing DeviantArt, Sotira says he realized artists of all types were interested in showcasing their work. He told the *Adweek* website:

> In 2000 I noticed that skinning your computer was becoming popular and there were artists moving in behind that development offering their skills. These artists . . . needed their own platform to publish their other art. So deviantART began by allowing these artists to publish original art and

news content to the web, collaborate with each other, comment on each other's artwork, build a fan base, and connect with third-party social networks to further promote the art. It expanded quickly past skins into the more than 2,500 categories of visual art that we have today.

Basic Research

Anyone considering potential businesses must evaluate what resources they would need to run their new enterprises. Money is one resource that may be in short supply. If they cannot or do not want to borrow money or obtain funds through investors, they need to focus on simpler ventures. This could include washing cars, mowing lawns, fixing computers, selling handmade clothing, or reselling thrift store finds through online auction websites.

Another resource that might be in short supply is time. The entrepreneur can choose to operate a new venture as a part-time business or as a full-time enterprise. Many people choose to begin a new business on a part-time basis, perhaps running it on the side while they work full time for someone else or attend school.

Regardless of whether they go into business full time or part time, no one should undertake a new business without doing some basic research. It is not enough to believe that a business concept under consideration is good and the product or service is needed. It is necessary to confirm these assumptions.

Would-be entrepreneurs can do some sleuthing to find out how similar businesses operate, what words and phrases they use to market themselves, and what customers have to say about those companies' strengths and weaknesses. An Internet search can quickly help identify the companies to study and offer some clues for how a new company might distinguish itself from others offering similar products or services. Websites used by consumers to post reviews, such as Yelp, Amazon, and Consumer Reports, can offer insights into what consumers value most and where they find existing products and businesses lacking.

To Patent or Not to Patent

Michelle Fisher heads Blaze Mobile, a start-up company that developed a smartphone app enabling users to pay for goods in a checkout line or buy tickets at a theater, sporting event, or concert hall by using their mobile devices. In 2005 Blaze Mobile sought a patent for the app.

Patents protect inventors from others who may try to profit from their inventions without their permission. But as Fisher learned, applying for a patent through the US Patent and Trademark Office can be a daunting process that can take years for the application to make its way through the approval process. In Fisher's case it took five years—a delay that nearly sunk her company. "Because it took so long for us to get our first patent, it became a problem for us as a small, self-funded startup," she wrote on the blog *IPWatchdog.com*. "As we waited for the patent to be granted, the . . . mobile payment market started to increase in activity. Big companies and well-funded startups began 'embracing' our ideas."

But Fisher said Blaze Mobile endured the wait and eventually won the patent. In the meantime, the company pursued additional mobile technologies and by 2014 obtained some 30 patents, with applications for 120 more pending before the US Patent Office.

Prospective business owners might even consider contacting the owners of some of those companies to ask questions and potentially benefit from their experiences. Companies that are at least 100 miles (161 km) away might not view the callers as potential competitors, which might make them more willing to discuss their experiences and even offer advice.

Understanding Customers' Needs

Basic research can also include working with a focus group. A focus group is often composed of a dozen or fewer people who are asked questions about a potential new product or service. By showing them the product or explaining the service and what it is expected to cost, entrepreneurs can get valuable feedback on whether or not they have an idea that resonates with others. Focus group members might come up with ideas that the businessperson should incorporate but perhaps would never have thought about. Their impressions on the product or service are recorded. Among the questions they may be asked are: Is the item or service usable? Is the item the right size? The right color? How much would they be willing to pay? How will the product or service improve their lives? Typically, focus group participants receive a small fee for their time—usually about fifty dollars.

> "The group was responsive, providing clear feedback on concepts as if talking to their best friend."
>
> —*Marketing manager Lisa Steckert, on the value of focus groups.*

Lisa Steckert, marketing manager for Honeywell Safety Products, a Smithfield, Rhode Island, company that makes protective eyewear, earplugs, and similar products, observed her first focus groups in 2014. She wrote on the website Research Access that on the day selected for the project, she observed four groups of seven individuals each for sixty minutes. A moderator led the groups, directing the conversations and soliciting opinions on products under consideration by the company. The focus groups met in a conference room equipped with a one-way mirror. Microphones and video cameras recorded each session. Sitting in the next room on the other side of the mirror, Steckert and other company officials observed the discussions. She says:

> I was fascinated by the attendants and surprised at how openly opinions were shared amongst the group. I expected people to be reserved, yet experienced the complete opposite. The group was responsive, providing clear feedback on concepts as if talking to their best friend. While I was uncertain how the research would go, by the end of the day I saw the value in this type of methodology. Understanding the "whys" behind something is very powerful. . . . After each session, we discussed potential "AHA" moments, questions to further probe on, areas of concern or praise, and overall "gist" of what took place and how to digest the information. Most importantly, we talked about what information is actionable and how.

Accessing Government Research

In addition to focus groups, there are many other ways to research the potential for products and services. Entrepreneurs can explore population trend data available through government agencies such as the US Census Bureau and US Bureau of Labor Statistics. For example, someone wishing to start a neighborhood business

Mining a Frustration

Twenty-seven-year-old Jess Edelstein is a big fan of organic health and beauty aids that don't use artificial colors or chemicals. She wanted to use a natural deodorant but was disappointed in the products she tried. So she created a new deodorant. Edelstein began by experimenting on herself before asking a longtime friend to take an early version of the deodorant with her as she spent a month volunteering in a tropical country. Her friend, Sarah Ribner, age twenty-six, reported that the deodorant worked well despite the humid South American climate.

Ribner and Edelstein started their own company, making a natural deodorant with charcoal, magnesium hydroxide, baking soda, and eleven essential oils. Appearing on the TV show *Shark Tank*, the partners took their PiperWai deodorant (the name is a combination of the name of Edelstein's dog and a tribe in the tropical and humid nation Guyana, where Edelstein worked as a teacher) concept to the investment professionals who are the show's stars. One of the investment pros decided to put $50,000 into their company, and viewers of the program pushed sales to $800,000. Most entrepreneurs do not appear on *Shark Tank*. But Ribner and Edelstein were prepared to take advantage of that opportunity because they had taken the time to research their product's effectiveness and desirability.

can determine how many people live in the area, their ages, typical incomes and education levels, what type of homes they live in, how long their commutes are, and other interesting facts. This information can be obtained by entering a zip code into the search engine at the US Census Bureau website, Census.gov.

Knowing these facts about the area would be helpful for companies that provide services to people who work and own their own homes. Or it may be helpful for business owners who anticipate looking for pools of potential employees. Companies that have a precise idea of what types of customers they will cater to—such as married people with incomes greater than $50,000—can hone in on communities to target their marketing efforts. Or somebody who is looking for a community in which to open a new pizza shop might be able to tell if a town or neighborhood has a particularly large population of young people—the type of customers expected to frequent pizza restaurants.

A second government agency, the Bureau of Labor Statistics, operated by the US Department of Labor, provides at-a-glance data for more than one hundred types of businesses. For example, business owners can discover whether the industry they are considering is gaining or losing jobs, what employees are typically paid, and other important trends.

After researching the marketplace through government agencies or by staging focus groups, and deciding on specific products or services to offer customers, prospective entrepreneurs are now prepared to take the next big step: to actually go into business. It could be a daunting challenge, but the smart entrepreneur has the advantage of doing the research and finding the business that fits perfectly into his or her lifestyle.

Chapter Three

Writing a Business Plan

Imran Merza conceived the idea for his company, Jealous Sweets, in 2010 when he started dating a girlfriend who was very picky about her diet. His girlfriend was a vegetarian who refused his offers of candy because many commercially made candies contain gelatin, which is composed of remnants from pigs, cows, and sheep. Merza wondered whether a market existed for candies that contain vegetable ingredients only. He wrote on the website Virgin StartUp, which helps entrepreneurs launch their new enterprises:

> Trying to impress my then-girlfriend at the start of our relationship, I started to look online and everywhere possible to see if I could find vegetarian sweets that I could give to her. I thought if I could make a premium brand of sweets taking out the gunk and junk [and] packaged, branded and marketed to grownups, sold in the places where sweets are not currently sold, then I could be onto something interesting.

Merza spent hours in public libraries, studying how candies are manufactured and marketed. He consulted with accountants, who helped him estimate what it would cost to start his own candy company. Finally, Merza wrote it all down—creating a business plan that outlined how he planned to establish and grow his company. He says, "Knowing what you want from the business and where you would like to take the business is vital because it gives you a track to run on, and that's why going through the process of writing a business plan is invaluable. It makes you think, and then think some more, about what you're doing. It ensures it actually makes sense."

> "Knowing what you want from the business and where you would like to take the business is vital because it gives you a track to run on."
>
> —Business owner Imran Merza.

Essentially, a business plan is a road map the entrepreneur follows as he or she begins and grows the business. The plan includes objectives and goals, a timeline, and an overview of the organization the entrepreneur expects to establish. Also, the business plan estimates the cost of running the business as well as the profit the entrepreneur hopes to earn.

Serving Two Purposes

Estimating the cost of running the business and the eventual profit earned by the business may be the most important points covered in the business plan. If the prospective entrepreneur hopes to raise money to start the business—either from investors or through a loan from a bank—the people who are going to be asked to finance the business will want to know how much it is going to cost and how much they should expect to earn for taking the risk. A business plan can help answer those questions.

Therefore, a business plan serves two purposes: It acts as a plan the entrepreneur can follow for the months or even years it may take to start and grow the business. Also, it serves as a blueprint to show potential investors or bank loan officers, explaining the products or services the business will offer as well as the anticipated costs and profits.

Business plans vary in length and complexity, often reflecting the nature of the venture being considered. A person who is starting a dog-walking business, for instance, might have a fairly simple plan, while a person who is opening a clothing boutique might need a more involved plan. Some business plans fill dozens of pages, while others amount to little more than a one-page explanation of the entrepreneur's goals. Although all business plans include some common elements, each plan should reflect the unique ideas of the business owner who writes the plan.

Executive Summary

The first important component of any business plan is the executive summary. This is a brief statement explaining the purpose of the business. In an article written for the website Bplans, which provides assistance in writing business plans, California software designer Tim Berry says the executive summary may be the most important part of the business plan, especially for someone who is trying to attract financial investors or obtain a loan. "Just like the old adage that you never get a second chance to make a first impression," Berry says, "the executive

> "The executive summary is your business's calling card. It needs to be succinct and hit the key highlights of the plan."
>
> —Software designer Tim Berry.

summary is your business's calling card. It needs to be succinct and hit the key highlights of the plan. Many potential investors will never make it beyond the executive summary, so it needs to be compelling and intriguing."

A sample executive summary provided by Bplans outlines the purpose and goals of a fictitious start-up company, Jolly's Java and Bakery:

> Jolly's Java and Bakery (JJB) is a start-up coffee and bakery retail establishment located in southwest Washington. JJB expects to catch the interest of a regular loyal customer base with its broad variety of coffee and pastry products. The company plans to build a strong market position in the town, due to the partners' industry experience and mild competitive climate in the area. JJB aims to offer its products at a competitive price to meet the demand of the middle- to higher-income local market area residents and tourists.

Organizational Overview

The next portion of the business plan is devoted to an organizational overview. This is a sketch of who will make the decisions, the jobs and duties assigned to the workers, and the equipment and supplies that need to be acquired.

The business owner would be expected to place him- or herself at the head of the organization, assuming authority for all decisions and strategies. If the business owner plans to be the only person in the organization, the owner should spell out the responsibilities he or she expects to take on to make the business work. The owner's education, experience in the field, and qualifications to manage the business should be addressed.

Do Investors Believe What They Read?

Before starting a software development company, Vivek Wadhwa wrote a business plan. He explains on the Bloomberg Business website:

> I was determined to lure professional investors, and I thought the key lay in creating lofty financial projections and carefully documenting the details. If all went according to my 40-page plan, my software company would be worth billions in five years by capturing just 1% of the market. My . . . friends told me that this was one of the most professional business plans they had seen.

But Wadhwa's plan failed to attract investors, and looking back Wadhwa finds himself questioning the value of business plans for start-up companies. Now an engineering professor at Duke University in North Carolina, he says:

> Over the years, I have mentored dozens of entrepreneurs seeking [investors] in their new companies and reviewed hundreds of business plans. They all seem to be the same. A startup business plan is always a good piece of fiction filled with great ideas. No one really believes what he reads in them. What [investors] look for before they make an investment is a proven product with strong market demand and an experienced management team.

If the business owner expects to hire employees, their roles are designated in the organizational overview. If the responsibilities of all employees are not clearly spelled out, it is possible the business may encounter troubles down the road. Perhaps too many employees were hired and some of them don't have enough to do, meaning the business owner could pay salaries to people who are idle for at least parts of their days. Or perhaps not enough employees were hired. Staff members may be too busy, which means the quality of their work may suffer or opportunities for growth are stifled because the business is limited in the amount of work it can take on. Therefore, potential investors or loan officers want to see a business plan address the need for employees and how the entrepreneur plans to utilize their time and talents.

The final element of the organizational overview should include a summary of what is needed to start and operate the business. Equipment needed to run the business should be listed. In the case of a business like Jolly's Java and Bakery, the owners may need ovens, kitchen appliances and baking implements, tables and chairs, and display cases. In addition, the entrepreneur may need office equipment and supplies—not only paper, stamps, and envelopes, but also desks and other furnishings, computers, printers, phones, and cash registers. If the business needs to lease space in a storefront or office, that information must be included in the organizational overview.

Marketing Plan

The next phase of the business plan is the marketing plan, which spells out how the business expects to attract customers. Before the entrepreneur gives thought to attracting customers, he or she needs to focus on identifying the customers. Thought must be given to the age, income, and geographic location of the customers. For example, teenagers would not be expected to hire a lawn-care company, but they would be expected to patronize a new pizza restaurant. Therefore, if the entrepreneur expects to sell pizza mostly to students, he or she may do well to look for a location near a high school or college campus. Deciding where to locate the business is a key element in marketing the business.

There are many different ways to attract customers. Some are very simple, such as placing printed fliers on the windshields of cars in a parking lot announcing the opening of a local pizza restaurant. Announcements of store openings or coupons can also be sent through the mail. In fact, the US Postal Service enables businesses to take advantage of low postage rates to send advertisements through the mail.

By researching the market while writing her business plan, Ann Rea found a unique way to attract customers to her new business. Trained as a commercial artist, Rea wanted to start a business producing and selling fine art paintings. As a resident of San Francisco, California, Rea knew that many vineyards are located in the nearby Napa Valley. She called several vineyard owners, asking if they had an interest in buying original landscape paintings that she would produce depicting their wineries. She found them to be quite enthusiastic—the vineyard owners planned to resell the paintings to their customers. "The wineries benefited because they got a permanent advertisement in someone's home," she told LivePlan, a company that assists entrepreneurs in writing their business plans.

With the growth of social media, many businesses have found Facebook, Twitter, and similar Internet outlets to be valuable tools to help with marketing. Business owners can post news and photos about their stores or companies. They can use social media to announce sales and provide links to their websites. Also, they can use social media to interact with customers—responding to comments or criticisms and answering questions.

Brandi Temple used Facebook to find thousands of customers for Lolly Wooly Doodle, a children's clothing company she established in 2008. As a young mother, Temple found herself dissatisfied with clothes that were designed for children—believing them to have too much of a grown-up look. "I wanted something that was cute for church that didn't cost an arm and a leg," she told the website Inc.com. "I wanted the kids to look wholesome and look their age."

Originally, Temple made all the garments herself, selling them to friends and neighbors in her hometown of Lexington, Kentucky. But in 2010 she started selling her garments on Facebook—posting photos and information on how to order the clothes. "I walked away from the computer and came back in like 30 seconds, and all the dresses were gone," she says.

Temple found she could not keep up with demand. Her customers were so enthralled with the garments they bought for their children that they shared the photos of the clothes on their own Facebook pages, which in turn were shared by their friends. Soon after she started selling on Facebook, she found the need to hire employees to make the clothes, and by 2012 the company was earning $11 million a year.

Financial Analysis

The final component of the business plan is the financial analysis. This is the section of the plan in which the entrepreneur totals up all costs of starting and running the business as well as providing an estimate of the profits the business is expected to earn. Investors and loan officers can be expected to pay particular attention to this portion of the business plan. If, in their view, the numbers don't make sense—perhaps they have concluded the entrepreneur has underestimated the start-up costs and overestimated profits—chances are they will refuse to invest in the venture. Or they may demand changes and require the entrepreneur to rewrite the business plan, providing new and more realistic estimates of costs and profits.

In addition to providing information to loan officers and potential investors, it is important for the business owner to include a financial analysis in the business plan to get a clearer picture of the economic burden he or she will be taking on. Moreover, potential employees will want to know the new business is on sound financial footing before they agree to take jobs there. Writing on the website Business Insider, financial journalist Martin Zwilling says, "In reality, you need to set these projections as goals for your own use, to convince employees as well as investors that you have a business which is challenging, but achievable."

> "You need to set these projections as goals for your own use, to convince employees as well as investors that you have a business which is challenging, but achievable."
>
> —*Financial journalist Martin Zwilling.*

Coming up with estimates takes time and thought. The owner needs to price equipment, supplies, and office furniture. Other costs—for transportation, support services (such as attorneys and accountants), and rental payments for storefronts or office space—must also be calculated. Employee wages must also be estimated in this section. All of these costs—salaries, equipment purchases, transportation, rental payments for store space, and so on—are known as overhead. This represents the costs entrepreneurs expect to incur to do business.

Accurate Projections

In writing the financial analysis, the entrepreneur must factor in all the overhead needed to run the business, weigh-

Envisioning a Business That Flourishes

Victoria Groves, an eighteen-year-old freshman at the University of Massachusetts, started her own desktop publishing business, providing newsletters, form letters, letterheads, business cards, and menus to clients. She named the business Letter Perfect.

Before starting, she wrote an eight-page business plan. She projected overhead—such as the cost of advertising as well as the cost of buying paper and ink cartridges. She also projected her income at $4,000 a year—a goal she did not manage to reach. Still, Groves says writing the business plan was an important step before seeking clients.

Groves told authors Frances A. Karnes and Suzanne M. Bean for their book *Girls and Young Women Entrepreneurs*:

> Writing a business plan helped me to learn a lot about myself. It forced me to sort out my ideas and think about questions such as: Where will I get the money to start this business? What will make my services better than those of my competitors? Is there a need for my services in the community? What price should I charge for each of my services? By answering these questions, I was able to envision my business flourishing and to anticipate some of the glitches that could occur.

ing those numbers against the value of the goods and services and how much customers can reasonably be asked to pay. A key factor in determining what to charge centers on the size of the profit the entrepreneur hopes to earn.

John Warrillow says he learned that figuring out the cost of overhead as well as a projected profit can be the most challenging aspect of writing a business plan and that for many new companies, there is simply no good way to estimate potential costs or profits. In 1996 Warrillow wanted to start a new magazine devoted to entrepreneurship. After researching the publishing industry, Warrillow proposed charging $99 a year for a subscription to his magazine, estimating that he would acquire ten thousand subscribers and earn nearly $1 million a year. To market the magazine to readers, Warrillow estimated that it would cost $10 per new subscriber. To start the magazine, Warrillow invested $17,000 of his savings.

The venture was a failure. After three months, Warrillow sold just eighty-two subscriptions and burned through his savings. Writing in the *Toronto Globe and Mail*, he says:

> The business plan I had spent months on was useless. It didn't matter how much time I spent modeling out a million-dollar company because the house of cards was all based on one wobbly assumption: my guess that it would cost $10 to acquire a subscriber. I had no basis for this assumption. I just made it up—which, of course, is the problem with the business plan of most start-ups: it's all fiction until you get into the market and start selling.

Warrillow's failure illustrates what could go wrong if a business plan does not make accurate projections for costs and profits. Moreover, if entrepreneurs do not give the proper thought or attention to the other aspects of their plans—the organizational overview and the marketing of their products or services among them—they may find themselves encountering many problems they may be hard-pressed to overcome.

Chapter Four

Raising Money

Some businesses can be started with virtually no money. A self-employed tutor, for example, provides only his or her knowledge of an academic subject to a client. A pet-sitter provides only his or her time to the job of looking after someone else's dog or cat. On the other hand, somebody who has an idea for a new sauce may need to purchase industrial-quality cooking equipment such as mixers, grinders, pots, pans, refrigerators, and a delivery truck that could cost tens of thousands of dollars. Or somebody who wants to start a more modest business like mowing lawns would still need to obtain equipment—mowers, trimmers, lawn edgers, and leaf blowers. Still, such equipment could easily cost $1,000 or more.

One of the earliest decisions a prospective entrepreneur needs to make is where to find start-up funding. The simplest option is to invest one's own money in the new business. This is called bootstrapping, and it can be accomplished by withdrawing money from personal savings accounts or by paying for needed items with credit cards. The latter strategy should only be used as a short-term loan, according to Marco Terry of Commercial

Capital LLC, a finance company that advises start-ups. He writes on the company's website, "If you elect to use your credit card, use it only for short-term situations in which you will be able to pay the credit card debt quickly."

Self-funding has both downsides and upsides. The downside of self-funding a business is that the entrepreneur assumes all the risk should the business fail. The upside is the entrepreneur does not have to share profits with anyone else. David Wu, who bootstrapped a digital marketing agency as well as other businesses, is convinced that working with one's own limited money makes for stronger management. He wrote on the *Forbes* website:

> With less capital to work with, you will be forced to start small, test your assumptions carefully, and then scale up. Along the way, you will learn about your products, markets and customers more intimately. And if you make mistakes—as all entrepreneurs do—they will almost certainly be smaller in scale and impact. Meanwhile, you will learn to become a scrappier, more vigilant founder.

"With less capital to work with, you will be forced to start small, test your assumptions carefully, and then scale up."

—Business owner David Wu.

Borrowing from Relatives

For more ambitious start-ups, personal savings may need to be supplemented with other people's money. This may come in the form of loans from relatives, a bank loan, or investors who are typically granted a percentage of the business in exchange for their capital.

When Mandy Baar learned the bakery where she worked as a college student was for sale, she at first did not see how she could afford to buy it. Nevertheless, she put together a detailed business plan, sharing it with family members as she sought their help to cover the down payment she needed to buy the bakery from the owner. Fortunately, several members of her family had confidence in Baar and lent her the money to buy the business. And while she paid them back—at an agreed-upon interest rate—she received something intangible from them as well. "The family members who loaned money to me have shown a lot of interest in my shop and they visit me and help out when I need assistance. I feel that I can ask them for advice when I'm struggling with a problem. As a single young woman, I've found this to be a good support system," Baar told the authors of *Girls and Young Women Entrepreneurs*.

Asking relatives for loans may prove difficult for all parties involved. The person making the request risks rejection from family members, while the relatives re-ceiving the request may feel uncomfortable saying no. In addition, should a loan be made but not paid back, family relationships could be irreparably damaged. Baar knew the risks but did not want to seek a loan from a commercial bank, perhaps because she knew that such loans can be difficult to obtain. That is especially true for someone with few assets or a less-than-perfect credit rating. People with poor credit may already carry a lot of debt. Or perhaps they have never attempted to estab-lish good credit by taking out loans, renting apartments, or applying for their own credit cards.

According to an index produced by the website Biz2Credit, in November 2015 large banks typically granted small business loans less than 23 percent of the time. Even small hometown banks are hesitant to grant most requests for business loans. During the same period, Biz2Credit reported, small banks granted loans to just 48 percent of applicants. "It's normal for business owners to have their first application [for a business loan] rejected," David Goldin, founder of business lender Capify, told the publication *Business News Daily*. "If anything, a rejection will alert an owner to the issues surrounding his business so they can make the changes necessary and move forward with a new application."

SBA Loans

New entrepreneurs may find they qualify for loans sponsored by the SBA. As with any other type of commercial loan, an SBA loan must be paid back with interest. The loan is not made by the SBA; rather, it is made by a participating bank under terms that are favorable to both the bank and business owner. When the bank grants an SBA loan, the government partially protects the lending bank from loss by guaranteeing repayments of 85 percent of the loan should the recipient's business fail. As for the borrower, he or she receives a lower interest rate than the bank would normally charge its commercial customers, because the federal government is providing protection to the bank, meaning the bank's risk is reduced because of SBA backing.

The most common SBA loan, designated by the government agency as the 7(a), can provide a business with up to $750,000. The money can be used to buy equipment and other assets and as working capital. Among the SBA loan options is the SBAExpress, so named because borrowers typically find out if they will receive the loan in less than two business days. Borrowers can apply for up to $350,000 through the expedited process. If a borrower wants less than $25,000, the bank making the loan is not required to ask for collateral. Collateral refers to assets that can be used to guarantee a loan. If a

What Is a Credit Score?

One factor banks employ to evaluate loan risk is an applicant's credit score, a number that ranges from 300 to 850. Credit scores reflect the financial responsibility of the borrower: A person with a high credit score typically pays credit card bills and loan payments on time.

The higher the credit score, the easier it is to secure a bank loan for a business at a favorable interest rate. Personal credit scores of 700 or above enable people to receive better receptions when they visit banks for loans. People with low credit scores may find themselves forced to pay higher interest rates because the bank believes they pose risks to repay the loans. Or they may be turned down for the loans altogether.

Before applying for loans, applicants should know their credit scores. It is a good idea to access one's own credit report before seeking a loan to be certain there are no errors that need to be corrected. Experian, Transunion, Equifax, and other credit bureaus supply credit reports upon request for a fee.

borrower fails to pay back the loan, known as a default, the bank can seize those assets. Assets often seized by the bank in the case of a default may be the mowers or vehicles owned by a landscaping company, the ovens and counters owned by a bakery, or the computers purchased by an entrepreneur who intended to write a new smartphone app. To recoup the money it is owed, the bank will liquidate those assets, meaning it will sell them and use the cash to satisfy the unpaid debt.

To apply for a loan backed by the SBA, borrowers have to go to a participating bank and fill out the required forms. Applicants need to indicate if they have ever been arrested or incarcerated and provide the lending institution

with a list of their assets, liabilities, sources of income, tax returns, and a projection of what they expect their new business will earn during its first year. Writing for the TV network Fox Business, business journalist Elaine Pofeldt says, "Applying for an SBA-backed loan may sound like a lot of work. It is—which has been a perennial source of frustration for small-business owners. But the pay-off is lower interest rates."

Microloans from Nonprofits

Microloans are made for smaller amounts of money than the typical SBA loan or commercial bank loan and must be paid back more quickly than other types of loans. As a result, microloans can be a better fit for many borrowers in start-up situations. The SBA has established a micro-loan program run on its behalf by a group of nonprofit companies. They are tasked with deciding who should receive loan money. The largest amount that can be borrowed is $50,000, and it must be paid back in no more than six years. According to the SBA, the average loan made through this program is for $13,000, which is typically paid back with interest in three years.

The SBA spells out what the money can and cannot be used for. For instance, it cannot be used to purchase land or buildings, but it can be applied toward working capital, inventory and supplies, furniture, and equipment. A list of nonprofits that are capable of making such loans can be found on the SBA's website. Each organization has its own rules and may charge differing interest rates, so potential borrowers should not assume they are all the same. Applicants may be asked to take business classes or work with SBA counselors before they receive approval for microloans.

When Rebecca Schulman wanted to start a business that would make gender-neutral baby gear, she applied to Accion U.S. Network, a nonprofit lending organization that participates in the SBA microloan program. Accion lent her $10,000 to help create prototypes, attend trade shows, and find suppliers. She agreed to pay back the $10,000 at an interest rate of 11 percent—which is a high rate compared to what a standard commercial loan may require. However, Schulman considered the rate fair because she had no track record as a business owner and therefore would probably not have been able to convince a bank to grant her a loan.

Crowdfunding

In recent years, thanks to the growth of the Internet and social media, many business owners have turned to crowdfunding to fund their ventures. Crowdfunding is the use of website platforms that link creative people with others willing to provide small contributions—typically fifty to one hundred dollars—to people whose ideas they find innovative and exciting. If enough people agree to crowdfund the idea, the entrepreneur may be able to raise tens of thousands of dollars to get a business started. Among the most popular crowdfunding sites are Kickstarter, Indiegogo, and GoFundMe. Each site has its own rules. For instance, Kickstarter only allows projects that fit within categories that include art, comics, dance, design, fashion, film and video, food, games, music, photography, publishing, technology, and theater.

According to Carol Tice, a *Forbes* contributor who has covered crowdfunding since its start in 2006, only about 41 percent of the campaigns that go live on Kickstarter reach their goal. Tice thinks many people mistakenly believe crowdfunding is a sure thing. She writes, "Crowdfunding platforms are not magical cash machines. They're simply a more efficient way for you to reach many potential backers than calling them on the phone or meeting them in person, one at a time."

Tice says there are five elements that lead to crowdfunding success. They include starting with a built-in audience of followers, admirers, and mentors; offering a product that is truly revolutionary; creating and executing a marketing campaign to lead people to the crowdfunding site; producing a professional-quality promotional video; and offering rewards people will be eager to receive.

> "Crowdfunding platforms are not magical cash machines. They're simply a more efficient way for you to reach many potential backers."
>
> —Writer Carol Tice.

Persistence Pays Off with SBA Loan

Mark Dost and two partners knew how to fix cars, but when they decided to go into business together, they wanted to try something new: a drive-through car wash. The Houston, Texas, residents needed to borrow money to buy the land for the car wash as well as cover the costs for constructing the building, equipping it, and running the business. Their requests for loans from local banks were turned down. Banks evaluate each business model that comes before them as they try to determine whether the borrowers will be able to pay back the loan. Dost and his partners found the banks judged the car wash industry as too risky. The banks determined the prospective company, Zoom Car Wash, was likely to fail—especially since none of the partners had experience running a car wash.

Undaunted, Dost and his partners persisted in their search to find a lender. They received approval from an SBA-affiliated lender that was more tolerant of risk because the government partially guarantees repayment of loans. Since opening for business in 2014, Zoom has been a success, and Dost and his partners are contemplating opening additional locations for new car washes.

One company that used Kickstarter successfully in 2015 is Houston, Texas–based 64 Oz. Games, whose fund-raising pitch was listed in the game category. Richard and Emily Gibbs established the company to produce dice featuring raised Braille patterns that could be used by sight-impaired people to play board games. The couple sought to raise $3,500 to purchase a 3D printer to make the dice.

The Gibbses ultimately raised more than double the amount of cash they sought, in donations ranging from ten to one hundred dollars from investors who thought the product was a good idea. To convince investors to offer start-up money, the owners produced a video about the company that showed the prototype for the Braille dice. In return for the donations, 64 Oz. Games offered various quantities of the dice to backers, depending on the level of support they provided. (Most crowdfunding sites require entrepreneurs to provide backers with goods for their donations, typically products that are produced through the crowdfunding efforts.) Unlike a loan, the Gibbses do not have to pay back their supporters, merely provide them with the goods they promised for their support. Had the company's level of support fallen short of its goal, they would not have gotten any money, a risk companies assume when they raise money through crowdfunding.

When it comes to securing the money they need to start their businesses, entrepreneurs must decide whether to self-finance, appeal to friends and family members, make their case to financial professionals such as bankers and microlenders, or appeal to the general public through crowdfunding. Although raising money for a new business is rarely easy, few entrepreneurs are able to pursue their dreams without financial resources. Therefore, prospective business owners would do well to prepare themselves for the rigors of raising money.

Chapter Five

Running the Business

Soon after Brian Casel started his software business in 2011, he found himself spending more time on administrative and clerical work than on developing software. Casel concluded that he needed to hire an employee to perform the mundane tasks of operating his business, freeing up his time for creative pursuits that would enable him to grow the company.

And so he hired his first employee. Writing on his company's website, CasJam, Casel recalls, "I started by giving her a few basic tasks, like formatting a blog post and posting to social media. That took about two hours. Then she [messaged] me, 'All done. What should I work on next?'" Casel paused to consider the question. He simply didn't have another assignment for his new worker. He certainly didn't want her sitting at her desk idle. And so he spent several hours finding work for her to do. Over the next several weeks, Casel says, it became clear to him that he did not have enough work for her and that he was spending too much of his time thinking up ways to keep her busy—which was hurting his company because he was unable to perform all the work he needed to do. Reluctantly, Casel fired his worker. "It was clear I would have to let her go," he says. "My first hiring experience was a failure. The worst part was that she was an excellent worker. The problem was my own doing. My business wasn't ready to support an employee. I wasn't ready to manage one."

Casel's experience illustrates that even after the large-scale planning is completed, the business plan is set, and the new business is launched, entrepreneurs face new challenges of running their businesses on a day-to-day basis. Among those challenges is knowing when and how to hire employees.

> "My first hiring experience was a failure. . . . The problem was my own doing. My business wasn't ready to support an employee. I wasn't ready to manage one."
>
> —Business owner Brian Casel.

Hiring and Retaining Employees

To find staff, business owners can rely on recommendations from people they know, advertise on the website Craigslist or similar job-posting sites, buy classified advertisements in newspapers, or even place help wanted signs in their business's windows.

In-person interviews should be conducted with applicants that seem most promising. Such meetings allow the business owner to gauge the job seeker's attitude, appearance, and punctuality. Experts suggest a variety of ways to ask questions. Many interviewers ask fact-based questions, posed to learn about past positions held by the candidate, length of service for their former companies, and the nature of the candidate's responsibilities. Those questions often provide good information, but Janis Whitaker, author of the book *Interviewing by*

Example, suggests interviewers can gain far more insight about candidates by asking what are known as behavioral questions. A typical behavioral question might be, "Can you tell me about a time when you initiated a project that resulted in increased productivity?"

Whitaker explains that behavioral interviewing is designed to gauge a candidate's prior successes because past performance is an excellent predictor of future performance. Therefore, the interviewer should seek specific examples that demonstrate skills. For instance, she says, instead of asking "Do you have initiative?" the interviewer would ask for an example of a time when the candidate demonstrated initiative. "In actuality you're not really asking someone if they have done something," Whitaker told the website Inc.com. "What you're doing is asking them to explain to you how they have done it. So it's very, very difficult to exaggerate or fake this interview."

Competitive Wages

Paying competitive wages could make it easier to attract and keep employees. In a restaurant, for example, the chef's salary would likely be higher than those of other workers because a chef is a highly skilled worker who has undergone special training and experience. A chef can expect to make twenty dollars or more an hour, while a dishwasher, who needs little in the way of training, may make minimum wage.

The federal minimum wage is $7.25, but some states have their own specific rates. Employers can find out what the industry wage averages are for specific job descriptions by visiting the US Bureau of Labor Statistics website.

Once the staff is in place, employers need to clearly state the expectations they have for each job and, if

Contract Basics

Whether someone writes a contract or signs one, the contract is regarded as a legal document whose basics should be understood by all parties. The website Find-Law, which provides legal resources for nonlawyers, outlines important points to consider when working with contracts. According to FindLaw, contracts should be written in easily understood language, with details fully spelled out as to delivery dates, methods of payment, and other details. A contract should contain a termination clause: a paragraph that addresses under what circumstances the parties—the people for whom the contract is binding—can dissolve the contract. Find-Law says:

> Contracts aren't meant to last forever, and if one party continually misses payments or fails to perform their duties, you want to have a mechanism in place so that you can (relatively) easily terminate the contract under these circumstances. It could be a mutual termination agreement (when the objectives of each side have been met through the contract), or more likely an agreement that either side can terminate if the other side violates a major term of the contract, after giving proper notice of its intent to terminate [usually 60 days].

necessary, provide the training the workers need to do their jobs. When an employee exhibits a poor attitude, fails to show up on time, or does subpar work, an employer needs to take quick action. If restating expectations for that employee's performance does not produce the required changes, the employer may need to fire the individual and find a new worker who does meet expectations.

Finding Suppliers

When a customer visits a Starbucks and orders a caramel brulée latte, for instance, that customer expects to be handed the sweet, frothy beverage in a cup bearing the company's logo. In the unlikely event that the Starbucks is out of ingredients to make the latte, customers would surely be disappointed. If that scenario happens often enough, customers might decide to take their business elsewhere.

As with the local Starbucks, all businesses need suppliers to deliver the ingredients necessary to provide the products they sell. New businesses need to carefully select the suppliers, or vendors, they want to do business with to make sure they find reliable ones that can meet their needs on time and at prices they can afford. To get started, business owners can make a list of suppliers they learn about through industry contacts, the Internet, and trade publications.

There are several types of vendors to consider. A business can buy directly through a manufacturer's representative. This option is used by bigger companies because it usually offers the best prices. Smaller businesses can buy supplies through distributors. Also known as wholesalers, distributors have already purchased the goods they sell and store them in their warehouses, ready to ship to customers. A third type of vendor includes craftspeople whose one-of-a-kind products can be purchased at trade shows or through independent representatives. A fourth type of vendor is the importer who arranges for US businesses to receive goods made in other countries.

Keeping Customers Happy

Once customers discover the business, an entrepreneur's goal is to keep them coming back. Moreover, business owners strive to provide a level of satisfaction to their customers that encourages them to recommend the business to their friends. Customers expect that promises made to them will be carried out promptly and that any problems that occur will be corrected quickly.

Problems are sure to arise, which Erik Kimel learned when he founded a tutoring company called Peer2Peer Tutors. He was only seventeen but had already learned a lot about entrepreneurship from his father, who was an experienced businessperson. "You can never win an argument with a customer. Ever," Kimel told author Kenrya Rankin for her book *Start It Up*. "Something is going to happen, someone is not going to be happy, and you're going to think that you're right. But it doesn't matter. You have to provide excellent customer service, and that means giving the customer what they're looking for—even if you take a hit on it. Your reputation is worth more than one transaction."

> "You have to provide excellent customer service, and that means giving the customer what they're looking for. . . . Your reputation is worth more than one transaction."
>
> —Business owner Erik Kimel.

One way to ensure that customers are happy is to ask for feedback. Customers will often offer great ideas if only the business owners take the time to ask. As general manager of FollowUp.cc, a tech company that markets an e-mail management system for business users, Suzanne Cohen reads her company's feedback closely. (By subscribing to the service, customers can take advantage of a feature that enables them to send comments to the company.) Cohen makes a point of reading and responding to all feed-

Once a business is up and running, owners need to make sure they keep their customers happy. Consistent quality of service and excellent customer relations are two important factors in running a successful business.

back, particularly the comments from customers voicing problems and concerns.

Cohen takes the position that if people complain they must have good reasons and that her company needs to improve. "The brutal honesty of our detractors has helped me see our shortcomings," Cohen wrote on the *Wootric Blog*, sponsored by a company that helps clients improve their customer relations. In some cases, Cohen says, she discovered that the level of service a client signed up for was not right for that person's business and advised the client to switch services—even if it meant using a cheaper service. In such cases, Cohen put customer service ahead of profits. She says, "Moral of the story: sometimes your worst critics actually love you. And they want you to help them stay in love with you by addressing their problems."

Growing Pains

In 2006, when he was in college, Nathan Nguyen started selling musical instruments under the name Instrumental Savings. Today the thirty-year-old entrepreneur runs a business consisting of a music store in Anaheim, California, as well as an e-commerce website. In building his business, he learned the value of persistence and going slowly.

Nguyen's first sale did not go as planned. Excited that he found his first customer, he failed to determine whether the customer could afford the instrument he wanted to buy. Nguyen gave the customer the musical instrument anyway, and when the customer failed to pay, he faced a $4,000 loss. However, he did not give up; instead, he resolved to be a better business owner. Nguyen spent a lot of money optimizing his website to draw customers to it. For three years he reinvested all profits in the enterprise. Instrumental Savings has been recognized as one of the top one hundred music dealers in the country by the National Association of Music Merchants, a trade group.

Maintaining Records

Business owners need to know how their businesses are doing so they may plan for the future and note problems before they become too large to fix. Completion of monthly financial statements provides key data that is akin to receiving a business report card. Income statements, cash flow statements, and balance sheets all have a place in monitoring a business's relative health.

Income statements take into consideration the money the business expects to make—its projected revenue—and compares that figure with its projected expenses. An income statement will record payment that is expected but has not yet been received. When revenue exceeds expenses, the business is profitable. When expenses exceed income, the business is operating at a deficit. Most businesses cannot sustain prolonged periods of losing money.

Cash flow is a term that describes how money "flows" to and from a business. A cash flow statement provides a look at the money that has actually been received; it is therefore a more accurate picture of what is happening than the income statement.

Balance sheets contrast what a company owns, known as its assets, against what it owes, which are known as liabilities. The difference between the value of assets and the amount of liabilities represents the company's net worth. If a company has more assets than liabilities, it has a positive net worth.

Take a Salary or Invest in the Business?

As the money starts coming in, business owners must decide what to do with it. They may elect to take some of the profits in salary or put the money back into the business to purchase more supplies and equipment. One person who faced that decision in 2004 was fourteen-year-old Blaine Mickens, who along with a friend began a landscaping business they called Estate Groomers. They didn't need much money to get it going—just a few dollars to print some business fliers and buy gasoline to power Mickens's father's lawn mower.

Soon the business grew to the point that they needed a second lawn mower. The boys found a cheap used mower at a local junkyard and got it running. Realizing the need to buy more equipment, Mickens didn't pay himself until he thought the business was on sound footing and equipment needs were met. Reinvesting the profits back into the business involves a short-term sacrifice for long-term gain.

Accountants and Lawyers

It may be necessary to retain the services of professionals for expertise the entrepreneur does not possess. The two most common professionals a small business might need are accountants and lawyers. Huge corporations often employ their own accountants and lawyers. Small businesses, however, may need these professionals only from time to time. Therefore, it is more common for small businesses to retain the services of accountants and attorneys on an as-needed, hourly basis.

Among the services an accountant can perform are looking for cost savings with vendors and employees, making sure financial transactions are recorded correctly, and managing payroll. The average hourly salary for accountants is thirty-one dollars.

Lawyers, who may charge $200 or more an hour, can be retained to handle specific problems as they arise, such as defending the business owner in a lawsuit or in negotiating the purchase or sale of a business. There are some services a lawyer could provide that business owners can usually perform themselves, after acquainting themselves with some commonly found resources. For example, an uncomplicated business contract may be crafted without an attorney's help. When signed by the appropriate parties, a contract is a legally binding document that spells out what the parties will do for each other. It contains three elements: an offer, the acceptance of the offer, and the amount of money that will change hands. Contracts may be used to confirm sales of goods and services, buy equipment, and rent office or retail space.

Paying Attention to Details

Starting a business can be exciting, yet running a business is full of everyday tasks that must be accomplished if the business is to thrive. The business owner needs to devote attention to tasks such as getting products out on time, maintaining quality, ensuring that adequate supplies are on hand, and paying bills. Moreover, if there are employees, the owner must ensure that the business is properly staffed and well managed. Clearly, handling all the details of running a business takes leaders who are passionate about their ideas, creative enough to negotiate the challenges ahead, detail oriented, and savvy enough to know when they need to hire other experts to provide the knowledge they lack.

Glossary

assets: Tangible property owned by individuals or businesses. Assets may include cash, inventory, buildings, and equipment.

bootstrapping: A term for self-financing a business. The name comes from a loop people would grasp to pull their boots on.

collateral: An asset people pledge to secure a loan.

deficit: The shortfall that occurs when a business's liabilities are greater than its assets.

entrepreneur: A person who creates a business with the intent of making money.

fliers: Simple one-page advertisements, sometimes printed on two sides, promoting a business or its products.

outsource: The act of having jobs that had been previously performed domestically moved to other countries where labor costs are cheaper.

overhead: Fixed essential costs for running a business that may include rent, salaries, utilities, and raw materials.

risk: The potential financial loss one could incur when taking a chance on a business.

vendors: People who supply ingredients businesses need to operate.

For Further Research

Books

Jack Canfield, *The Success Principles: How to Get from Where You Are to Where You Want to Be*. New York: Morrow, 2015.

Daniel R. Castro, *Hidden Solutions All Around You: Why Some People Can See Them and Some Can't*. Austin, TX: Beartooth, 2015.

Raia King, *From Daydream to Dream Job: Make Money Being Creative*. Exton, PA: London Media, 2012.

Steve Mariotti, *The Young Entrepreneur's Guide to Starting and Running a Business: Turn Your Ideas into Money*. New York: Crown Business, 2014.

Barry Thomsen, *The Smart Guide to Starting Your Own Business*. Norman, OK: Smart Guide, 2012.

Periodicals and Internet Sources

Drake Baer and Richard Feloni, "9 Legendary Entrepreneurs Who Started When They Were Kids," Business Insider, November 27, 2014. www.businessinsider.com /entrepreneurs-who-started-their-first-business-as -kids-2014-11.

Maggie Blaha, "You're Never Too Young to Be CEO," CNN, December 10, 2014. www.cnn.com/2014/05/19 /living/kid-entrepreneurs-irpt-schools.

Linda Lloyd, "Young Restaurateur Opens Ninth Friendly's Franchise," *Philadelphia Inquirer*, December 22, 2015.

Elizabeth Palermo, "10 Things That Could Keep You from Getting a Small Business Loan," *Business News Daily*, April 16, 2014.

Deena Varshavskaya, "4 Practical Ways to Find Your Life's Passion and a Career You Love," *ForbesWoman*, July 2, 2014.

Ryan Westwood, "How to Fund a Business with Kickstarter," *Forbes*, July 1, 2015.

Websites

Biz Kid$ (www.bizkids.com). The website of the public television series by the same name. Watch clips from the shows that combine business concepts with entertainment, download a business plan form, and read the blog to explore what young people need to start their own business and learn about money and finances.

Entrepreneur (www.entrepreneur.com/magazine). The website of the monthly print magazine *Entrepreneur* contains stories written by contributors on virtually every aspect of starting and running a business, including social media, growth strategies, marketing, franchises, technology, and leadership.

SCORE (www.score.org). The website links entrepreneurs to ten thousand experienced volunteer mentors who can provide them with custom business advice in person or online. In addition, the site features articles on topics such as starting and running a business, growing an enterprise, finances, and management.

US Small Business Administration (www.sba.gov). The official website of the government agency provides comprehensive information on starting a business and understanding markets, business data, and types of businesses. There are many resources specifically for young entrepreneurs, including the online course Young Entrepreneurs: An Essential Guide to Starting Your Own Business.

Online Tools, Games, and Apps

Check Domain (www.checkdomain.com). A quick way to find out if a domain name is taken, by country, by typing in the desired domain name into the website's search box.

Entrepreneur Game (ttps://play.google.com/store/apps /details?id=com.santander.emprende). The free app lets players create and manage a web design company performing functions such as hiring, advertising, budgeting, and project management. There are three cases and three levels of difficulty to work through.

Stock-o-Mania (www.learn4good.com/games/tycoon business/entrepreneurgame.htm). The online game lets players turn their own small businesses into international powerhouses through buying and selling fruits and vegetables, oil, wheat, cotton, and other goods. If they are savvy, players can acquire businesses in six states.

Index